The Ultimate Wedding Savings Guide

How to Plan the Wedding of Your Dreams Without Breaking the Bank

April Hall

This book is dedicated to the newly engaged couple. Use the suggestions and planners provided in this book to create your dream wedding while staying within your budget.

Copyright Act of 1976, the scanning, uploading and electronic sharing of any part of this book without the explicit written consent or permission of the publisher constitutes unlawful piracy and the theft of intellectual property.

If you would like to use material or content from this book (other than for review purposes), prior written permission must be obtained from the publisher.

You can contact the publishing company at admin@speedypublishing.com. Thank you for not infringing on the author's rights.

Speedy Publishing LLC (c) 2014
40 E. Main St., #1156
Newark, DE 19711
www.speedypublishing.co

Ordering Information:
Quantity sales; Special discounts are available on quantity purchases by corporations, associations, and others. For details, contact the "Special Sales Department" at the address above.

This is a reprint book.

Manufactured in the United States of America

Table of Contents

Publisher's Notes i

Chapter 1: Introduction 1

Chapter 2: Congratulations on Your Engagement! Time to Start Planning 3

Chapter 3: Wedding Apparel 13

Chapter 4: How to Cut Costs At the Reception 21

Chapter 5: Don't Rely on Friends and Family for Video & Photography 36

Chapter 6: Planning Your Honeymoon 40

Chapter 7: Your Planning Timeline 47

Chapter 8: Wedding Resources 50

Meet the Author 54

More Books by April Hall 56

Publisher's Notes

Disclaimer

This publication is intended to provide helpful and informative material. It is not intended to diagnose, treat, cure, or prevent any health problem or condition, nor is intended to replace the advice of a physician. No action should be taken solely on the contents of this book. Always consult your physician or qualified health-care professional on any matters regarding your health and before adopting any suggestions in this book or drawing inferences from it.

The author and publisher specifically disclaim all responsibility for any liability, loss or risk, personal or otherwise, which is incurred as a consequence, directly or indirectly, from the use or application of any contents of this book.

Any and all product names referenced within this book are the trademarks of their respective owners. None of these owners have sponsored, authorized, endorsed, or approved this book.

Always read all information provided by the manufacturers' product labels before using their products. The author and publisher are not responsible for claims made by manufacturers.

Chapter 1: Introduction

Congratulations! You're getting married! Or, in the very least, you're dreaming about getting married.

This book will help you to plan the perfect wedding while saving you a lot of money no matter when you're tying the knot. You should be applauded for researching all there is to know about wedding planning. After all, your wedding day is one of the biggest events that will ever happen to you in your lifetime! You should make it special. It ranks right behind Sweet sixteen, eighteen, high school prom, graduation and the twenty-first birthday!

It's natural for you to feel a little anxious when you think about planning a wedding. You're wondering right now what is the best way to celebrate. Get ready. Planning a wedding can be one of the most challenging times for couples. EVERYONE will have an idea on what you should do and how you should do it.

The only way that matters is your way! You and your fiancé are the only two people who matter. Plan your wedding your way. In the end, you can sing the old Frank Sinatra song. No matter what happens, you did it your way.

This is an exciting time for you. You have found the one person that you can't live without and want to spend the rest of your life with. The rest of your life is a long time but nevertheless, you've found that special someone.

The question is now what do you do? Plan, plan, and have fun planning some more! Once the plan is set, stop worrying! You're going to make a wonderful bride and groom.

Let's get you ready for your journey down the aisle.

Chapter 2: Congratulations on Your Engagement! Time to Start Planning

Wedding Savings Trend #1

Couples are choosing to get married on Thursday, Friday or Sunday nights. Those days are less expensive than Saturday weddings.

Saturdays have been the wedding day of choice for years. But a new day is dawning. Folks have figured out that it's cheaper to get married on Thursdays, Fridays and Sunday nights. Sunday nights before a long holiday weekend is the most popular. The Fourth of July is also a big choice.

THE PRE-PLANNING STAGE

It's not too early to start thinking about what day you want to get married on. It's cheaper to get married on any other day EXCEPT Saturday. You'll have to make the decision if any other day will work for you. It's understandable if you're hell bent on getting married on a Saturday because it has been historically the most common wedding day.

During the pre-planning process you need to determine a wedding budget. You'll decide on what you can afford and what you can't. You'll decide on the things you must have versus the things you can live without. You may not think you can afford all the lavish things you want for your wedding, but the goal of this book is to show you ways to make things more affordable.

That's it in a nutshell. The key to planning a wedding on a budget is deciding on what you want to spend a whole lot on. You have to decide what things you won't skimp on. Most couples have one thing in common when it comes to wedding planning. They all want a memorable event. There are many ways you can do this as well.

Planning a wedding is a huge undertaking. There are several areas that will need your concentration if you're going to save bit money on your wedding costs. You and your fiancé will need to determine what is a priority for you as a couple.

You'll need to determine if there are certain things specific to the wedding that you must have. It could be that you want a certain band to play or a certain color to wear. It could be a certain location for the wedding or reception. For example: A couple wanted their wedding to be at an exclusive resort. The wedding chapel was in the midst of a garden beyond belief. The couple spent a ton on money on the location but they also saved a lot of money because they didn't have to buy flowers. Once you determine your must haves, you can then begin to incorporate them into your wedding.

EIGHT AREAS WHERE YOU CAN SAVE THE MOST

There are eight areas where you can save the most on wedding costs. Here they are:

1. Food
2. Bar

3. Wedding Attire
4. Flowers
5. Photography & Videography
6. Music
7. Honeymoon
8. Guest List

Look at these areas and start thinking in the cost saving mode. Food and bar costs are one of the biggest expenses you'll have. You may decide to have a buffet or cater the reception yourself. You may decide to have an open bar for an hour or not to serve alcohol at all. These are all cost saving measures that you will want to think about.

The location where you're going to have the reception is also a big expense. Parks, forest preserves and a home backyard are all viable options for you. You'll see that wedding attire is on the list of the areas where you can save the most money. As you go through the wedding planning process, you'll want to keep an eye out for discounted wedding attire.

You can also find some great deals on flowers if you know how to look and know what you're looking for. Included in the book is a list of more than 250 flowers and plants to help you decide on what you want. A wedding wouldn't be a wedding without the romantic mood that only flowers can provide.

The photographer and videographer is on the list of biggest expenses. You want to capture as much of your wedding as possible and should hire professionals to accomplish this. But, there are ways to skimp without missing out on the memories.

Everyone who is anyone will want to attend your wedding! It's inevitable that someone is going to be disappointed because they were not invited. However, keeping a tight lid on your guest list is very important to living within a budget. A good rule of thumb is not to invite more guests then you can spend a minute with.

CAN YOU BE YOUR OWN WEDDING CONSULTANT?

Do you need a wedding consultant? A wedding consultant is responsible for helping to plan the wedding from the beginning to the very end. Theoretically, you can do this yourself. Some people save money by having a wedding consultant only on the day of the wedding. I believe this is a good way to save money as well.

A lot of times a church, reception hall, hotel and other venues will provide you with a wedding consultant on the day of the wedding as part of your package. Some other wedding consultants charge as much as 15% of the total money spent on the wedding. It's a good idea to go with a wedding consultant who is affiliated with a professional wedding organization. Some of these organizations are listed at the back of the book.

COORDINATING A WEDDING

Your plans should be the best-case scenario. You've heard the old saying what the mind can conceive and believe; it can achieve?

Get a pen and paper ready. Sit back, relax and envision what the perfect wedding for you would look like. Go through every detail from the colors that your attendants are wearing to the time of day it is. Imagine what your dress will look like and where the reception will be.

Now, you're ready to begin the exciting process of wedding planning. You'll need a three ring binder, loose-leaf writing paper and notebook dividers with tabs. You'll proceed to organize all of the information you'll gather in the coming weeks and months ahead in this notebook.

Here's the headings you'll need for every section in your notebook.

1. Calendar
2. Budget
3. Clothing
4. Ceremony
5. Flowers
6. Decorations
7. Reception
8. Food
9. Videography/Photography
10. Guest/gift list

DEVELOPING A BUDGET

The budget is important for obvious reasons. You don't want to end up spending yourself into a divorce before you're even married. A budget gives you strict guidelines to follow. Overspending will not necessarily give you the wedding of your dreams. The idea is to do it well without emptying out your bank account.

This gives you an idea of what your budget should look like percentage wise. Take a look at it.

1	Reception	50%
2	Bride's Dress, Shoes, Garter	15%
3	Videographer/Photographer	10%
4	Music	10%
5	Flower	10%
6	Decorations	2%
7	Invitations/thank you cards	2%
8	Postage	1%
		100%

You may be thinking; so many decisions, so little time. You'll need some help along the way. Solicit any and everybody you care about to help you. There are several things you'll need to do right away.

Here they are:

1. Meet with parents
2. Pick a date
3. Reserve the ceremony and reception locations
4. Pick your wedding party
5. Meet with minister or rabbi
6. Choose a color theme and scheme
7. Begin guest list
8. Select a wedding dress, mother's dresses and bridesmaid dresses

One decision you'll also have to make is whether you'll need a wedding consultant. You can save money if you decide to plan your wedding without one.

THREE TRADITIONAL THEMES

A budget may be the first thing a wedding coordinator will want to go over with you. But, a wedding theme is the second. You don't have to have one, however a wedding theme can give you some direction and creativity with your planning. For instance; a themed wedding where the couple plays out Cinderella complete with glass slipper and horse drawn buggy. None of the bridesmaids fit the glass slipper. Very cute. Take a look at the themes below to get some ideas.

Rose Riches

As its name suggests, roses, roses and more roses make up the theme to this wedding. The idea is to buy as many as you can afford, then fill in the gaps with lots of greenery. If you can beg, borrow and steal from relatives to get the potted plants out of homes and backyards you'll save a lot of money that way. You can also use ribbons in the color scheme that you're using to tie around the plants. You can even add silk plants in with the live ones to add a dramatic effect. You can add wrought iron benches to create the garden affect as well.

In The Park

This theme is as its name suggests. You can pick a park to get married in and ship in more and flowers as needed. You can add in candle towers to portable streetlights at night to create the desired effect.

Hearts Mixed With Flowers

You'll want to use lots of hearts all over the place with this theme. You can buy many different kinds of heart shaped items in your local party store. If you're really looking to save money, you can make your own.

EIGHT NONTRADITIONAL THEMES

Non-traditional theme weddings often have one thing in common. Elaborate costuming and dramatic effects. Let's take a look at eight of the most common nontraditional weddings.

All Hallow' Eve

Halloween is a favorite event for a lot of people including kids. It's not odd that once your grow up that you'd want to get married on one of your most favorite occasions, right? Halloween weddings include costumes and a masquerade ball type of event. You can downplay the harsh orange and black colors of Halloween by mixing in other colors like grays, silvers and white. Consider using pumpkins with smiley faces as table decorations. Orange and black candles also create a lively affect.

Balloons

Balloons can create the same dramatic affect that flowers cans. You can hang them in the doorway to the reception or wedding hall. You can tie them to chairs. You can even use the bouquets on the tables as centerpieces. ou can take your pick, cover the ceiling with a helium blown balloon or cover the floor with a hot air blown balloon. The idea is to have balloons everywhere! This is a very cost effective theme.

Celtic

Celtic weddings are booming right now. They are similar to renaissance weddings in that you'll need an old castle or outdoor setting in order to pull it off. The bride wears an ivory satin gown and a flowered wreath. The groom wears plaid tartans, kilts and kneed high white socks.

Country 'N Western

Get your blue jeans and line dancing shoes ready. You're in for a foot stomping, hand clapping good time. The food for the day is barbeque and potato salad. The reception hall is lined with red and white-checkered tablecloths. You can pull this theme off on a real life ranch or outside in a big backyard. Let your imagination run wild as far as decorations are concerned. You can use anything from cowboy hats to red bandanas. Let's move from the old west to the south of the border.

Fiesta

Have fun planning a Mexican fiesta! This theme is for people who enjoy the culture and the people. You can enjoy authentic Mexican food including tacos and burritos. You can also have fun decorating using piñatas and paper crepe flowers. Perhaps the warmth of Mexico isn't your only option. Try a wedding theme that takes you across the Pacific.

Polynesian

Okay, so you may not be able to duplicate the Pacific Ocean for a Polynesian wedding. Any body of water will do! All you need are authentic music, tiki torches, flower leis and crepe paper flowers to get you in the mood here. The food is relatively inexpensive including from roast pork to fresh fruit.

Renaissance

Renaissance weddings are similar to a Celtic wedding in that you'll need elaborate costuming. They also take place outside or on the grounds of an old castle. The bride wears a heavy gown similar to what they use to wear in the 14th century. It has bell shaped sleeves and a V back line. The groom and his groomsmen wear velvet doublets and shirts with billowing sleeves. A feathered hat and sword tops off the man of the hour's wardrobe.

The Ole South

This is another wedding theme that takes place mainly outdoors. You'll need a beautiful mansion or plantation to help pull this theme off. The bride wears a southern belle wedding dress complete with parasol. The bridesmaid's dresses are also ball gowns. The groom and his groomsmen wear white dinner jackets and black pants.

10 ETHNIC RITUALS

Once you decide what theme you want, it will become easier to plan some events around that theme. Did you know that some themes reflect your ethnic heritage? Well it does. Let's take a quick look at how ethnicity is connected to us.

1. African American couples celebrate what's called a "jumping of the broom." This happens immediately after the "I do's."

2. Chinese couples drink wine from goblets that are tied together with a red ribbon.
3. East Indian grooms get a turmeric paste rubbed all over their face to keep the bad spirits away.
4. German brides carry salted bread in their pocket and the groom carries grain to bring wealth into the household
5. Egyptian brides get their right wrist tied to the grooms left wrist.
6. English brides get a live or imitation spider placed in their gown by their guests.
7. French couples drink wine from a two cup that has two handles.
8. Greek brides receive money pinned to their gowns while dancing with her new husband during the reception.
9. Italian grooms get their ties cut into small pieces. The pieces are sold to the guests.
10. Korean couples feed their guests noodle soup to symbolize a happy life together.

These are just some of the rituals that are performed based on ethnicity. Did you recognize any of them? Do you want to include any of them as part of your wedding celebration? You can really make your wedding unique by incorporating a ritual.

CHAPTER 3: WEDDING APPAREL

Wedding Savings Trend #2

Couples are saving money by buying wedding cakes, flowers and reception food from the local supermarkets.

Well, who would've "thunk" our Wedding Saving Trend #2? Research shows that couples are flocking to the local grocer for wedding finger food like chicken wings and cheese crackers. They are also saving money over catered prices for salads, vegetable platters, etc. Cake is the biggest buy. You can save at least 15% by buying your wedding cake depending on the size from a supermarket.

We'll talk a little bit more about how to save on wedding reception costs a little later. But, for right now, let's talk about saving money on one of the most important stars of your wedding.

MEET THE KEY PLAYERS

Talk to any wedding consultant and they will tell you. There are several key people that you'll need to pull your wedding off. Of course, your parents will be on hand to help if they can. The minister is also important. However, your wedding party is very, very important.

Next to you, they are the people everyone is going to be gazing at. What do they have on? How is the hair and makeup styled? Shoes, do the shoes match perfectly? These are all questions your guests are going to ask as they watch your wedding party parade up and down the aisle. So of course, these are the key players aka stars.

1. Matron or Maid of Honor
2. Best Man
3. Groomsmen
4. Bridesmaids

Now, let's look at how they are supposed to assist you in the days leading up to D-Day.

The Matron or Maid of Honor is the bride's right hand woman the wedding day. She helps the bride get dressed. She distributes the corsages and boutonnieres. She fixes the bride's train during the ceremony. She is the official witness to the vows. But, her duties actually begin long before then. She helps to address invitations and thank you notes.

The Best Man is the groom's right hand guy. He is in charge of making sure everything and I mean everything runs smooth. He is the official witness to the vows, however he has many more duties. He pays the clergy He handles the groom's travel, supervises ushers, holds the rings and marriage license, and delivers the toast.

The Groomsmen on the other hand have many duties on the wedding day. They are usually the first people who guests see when they come to the wedding. It is their duty to meet and greet the guests. Seat them on the proper side of the church aisle if there is one. Groomsmen also seat the bride and grooms mothers. In some cases, groomsmen also arrange for the transportation of the bridesmaids. Now, if your wedding is so big that you're having groomsmen and ushers, then it is up to the ushers to seat the guests.

The Bridesmaid's main duty is to look pretty and happy on the wedding day! No joke. If you're a bridesmaid, consider the job a piece of cake. You'll get to run errands for the bride or her mother in the weeks before the wedding, but aside from that, being pretty is their sole responsibility.

THE WEDDING ATTIRE

You can help your wedding party look good by finding dresses, tuxedos and other attire that compliment them. You should look at the color, style, fit and feel of the material as well. You'll also want to keep in mind the theme of your wedding that we talked about in Chapter One. Let's look at how we can save money on wedding attire.

Save Money by Renting

I know you're wondering. Rent a wedding dress? It's not as strange as it might seem. A lot of brides are saying to themselves. Will my daughter really want to wear my wedding dress at her wedding 20-30 years from now? More than likely, NOT! It uses to be a grand tradition to get married in white, and spend several hundred dollars to preserve a wedding dress. However, more brides are opting not to wear mom's old wedding dress.

Buy a Prom Dress

Who can really tell if a prom dress is a prom dress? Prom dresses like wedding dresses are all formal. In addition, prom dresses are usually priced lower than the dresses that are slated for weddings. Don't ask why, that's just how the designers, retailers do it. Look at the prom dresses before you order dresses for your wedding party. You may be in for a big surprise.

WHAT KIND OF DRESS?

You have your choice of buying the dresses for your wedding or renting. Let's look at what kind of dress would be right for your wedding. You have been thinking about your wedding dress more than likely since you were a little girl. Now is the time to start really looking for one. Before you can decide what kind of dress you want to buy, you have to first decide on what kind of wedding you are going to have.

Remember, the exercise from Chapter One where you were asked you to envision your dream wedding. If you completed that exercise then more than likely, you know what you want your dress to look like. But, hold on, let's make sure your idea of a dress matches up with the kind of wedding that you are going to have.

FORMAL/INFORMAL OR NOT

Are you planning on having a formal, informal wedding or something in between the two? Do you want to bare your midriff and make a fashion statement or do you want to take a trip into medieval times. Do not laugh. You may remember from Chapter One that Celtics and Renaissance weddings are among the most common theme weddings. Some people have wonderful wedding celebrations of this kind.

Getting back to you. You may not know what kind of wedding you are going to have just yet. After all, we are just in Chapter Two. You may not know what kind, but you have a good idea of how you want it to look. I believe you will also know the general vicinity of where you want it held. You may even have your guest list sketched in your brain. Whatever is the case, it is a thin line between a formal versus an informal wedding. Let us look at the two.

Formal Wedding

A formal wedding is usually a religious ceremony that takes place at church, cathedral, synagogue, chapel or other worship place. You can have a full reception with assigned, sometime unassigned dinner seating after the wedding. The reception can take place at a variety of places including a country club, museum, hotel, cruise ship, etc. The groom and groomsmen are decked out in tuxedos, suits or other formal wear.

A formal wedding requires the bride to wear either a white, or off-white floor length gown. The train should be cathedral or chapel length with a train about the same size.

Semi Formal Weddings

Semi formal weddings take place at either a chapel, garden, scenic or private home. A semi formal reception can take place at a variety of buffet style or it can be catered under a tent. The bride's gown can be white, off white, or pale pastel. The length of the dress can vary from ankle length to knee length.

The bride can skip wearing a train with a semi formal wedding. You can wear a long or short veil depending on the style of the dress. The groom can dress in a tuxedo or suit. The groomsmen must wear matching clothes. Semi formal wedding skip traditions like a receiving line and announced introductions.

The Informal Wedding

An informal wedding is basically any wedding that is not formal or semi-formal. It can happen anytime, anyplace. You set the stage to make the wedding out of the norm.

The informal wedding is usually short, sweet and very, very, personal. Sometimes no one else is there but the bride and groom. As you can see, it is very important to decide what kind of wedding you are going to have when you are looking for a gown.

Time of Year

Winter is not the most popular time of year to get married. Yet, there are some people who do not mind the cold and snow. You will want to make sure you are following the standards based on the time of year. For instance, for a wintertime wedding you will want to wear long sleeves and a higher neckline to help you stay warm. There used to be a time when wearing strapless gowns in the middle of winter was a fashion no. But, times have changed and now it is okay as long as you are warm. Fur, muffs, boots and gloves are also okay for a bride to wear at a winter wedding.

Fall weddings are beautiful with the falling leaves as a backdrop. A bride may want to choose a gown made out of a medium weight fabric like taffeta or raw silk. Sleeves on the dress are usually kept at three quarter length for a fall wedding. You will want to have a lightweight train. A shawl to help keep the wind off your back.

Spring weddings give the bride to be a chance to show off her style and grace. It is not unusual to see a bride with a pillbox hat on in lieu of a veil. The gown can be made out of a silk tulle, or organza material. A tea length to longer length is also okay depending on what you like. You can also wear cap sleeves or an off the shoulder neckline. It is also okay to pull out the open toed shoes are also okay for a spring wedding.

Summer is the most popular time for nuptials. You have a variety of dresses and fabrics to choose from if you go with this time of year. You can have your pick from short, medium, and ankle length dresses. You can also find styles from halter to backless. The fabric comes in anything from linen to tulle. Thinking about not wearing a veil! Go ahead. Summer is the time of year for a bride to be bold and beautiful. You can wear a flower headpiece to a wide brimmed straw hat. Some brides also opt to go barefoot to sandals.

Follow Your Style

Let's set aside for a moment the discussion over what size you are and what dresses look best on you. Let's talk about you following your own natural style. You can get married in a wedding dress that reflects the usual essence of you if you know what to look for.

You may be a fancy dresser who loves clothes that flair. If so, then your wedding dress should flair as well. On the other hand, if you are more conservative in your everyday attire, then you'll want a sleeker look for your wedding. You're just following your own sense of style this way

How Much to Pay?

This is a big question! Some people will bargain shop until they find the nicest dress for the most affordable price. Still, there's another school of thought that suggests your wedding dress should be the most expensive dress you'll ever own. In other words, the sky is the limit when you want a wedding dress.

You may want to look again at the general wedding budget located Chapter One. As you can see, the dress, headpiece/veil, lingerie, shoes and accessories fall in the 15% range for your wedding expenses. However, I say feel free to play around with the numbers. If you can cut corners in other areas, by all means please do. Designer wedding dresses are the most expensive. They range in price from $1,500 on up. However, you may be able to find a wedding dress on sale for as little as $300.00.

On an average, brides are spending about $800.00 for their dresses. You can also save some money be wearing your mother or grandmothers wedding dresses. Yes, people are still doing that.

Bear in mind if you go the "something old" route you will most likely have to pay a little extra for alterations.

A TUX FOR HIM

Okay! That's enough about the female persuasion for right now. Let's talk about attire for him. It's important as well, you know. Let's face it! The man's attire is not as important in a wedding as the woman's attire. However, tuxes are an important side issue. More and more people are opting to buy tuxes because they figure they'll use them over again during the course of a marriage.

They guys play an important role in a wedding. They are the first people your guests see. Be sure to pick out a tux that conveys the tone of your wedding.

Rent or Buy?

I bet you were wondering how you should handle the question over tuxedos. Should you rent or buy is another good question. Tuxedo's like a wedding and bridesmaids dresses help to set the tone for your overall wedding. Tuxedo's cost anywhere from $300.00 to $500.00 depending on where you buy them. You will pay about 30 percent of the price of a new tuxedo if you rent a tuxedo.

To Suit or Not To Suit

A lot of grooms are saying to heck with tuxedos. They are going for the idea of wearing a fine suit on their wedding day. Picking a suit over a tux for a formal wedding is a growing idea. If your guy is not a fan of tuxedos, a black on black suit can and will give him the same dashing effect!

CHAPTER 4: HOW TO CUT COSTS AT THE RECEPTION

Wedding Savings Trend #3

You may have not heard about this trend because it's so hot off the market! A member of your family or a friend can become temporarily ordained in order to marry you! Hey, don't laugh; you could save in ministerial costs on this one.

Okay, so having your Uncle Bob marry you may not be your cup of tea. Saving money on your wedding isn't just limited to the wedding itself. The bulk of your savings will come from cutting the costs at your wedding reception.

The time of day that you hold your wedding and reception also plays an important role. Take a look at the timetable below. You can save a pretty penny by having your wedding during a time of day when folks are not "as hungry".

Morning Wedding Ceremony before 11:00am
Continental breakfast or buffet

Midday Wedding 11:00am to 1:00pm
Luncheon buffet

Afternoon Wedding 1:00pm to 4:00pm
Hors d'oeuvres buffet or cake and punch only

Early Evening Wedding 4:00pm to 7:00pm
Dinner buffet

Evening Wedding after 7:00pm
Hors d'oeuvres buffet or cake and punch only

As you can see, the amount of food you'll need to supply at your wedding reception depends on the time of day you hold your reception. Let's now look at the ways you can save in a nutshell! Here's how to do it and do it big! Save as much as 40-60% on your reception costs by following this advice.

Below are the top ten ways to save money on your reception:

SERVE NON ALCOHOLIC DRINKS
You can save a fortune by only serving non-alcoholic drinks like sparkling cider or grape juice at your wedding reception. Other couples just serve wine or champagne. In those cases, you can still save money by buying your alcohol in bulk.

BUY LIQUOR WHOLESALE
You may decide to go the extra mile and give your guests the option to drink if they want. One way to do this and save money along the way is to buy your liquor direct from a wholesaler. A wholesaler will offer you a discount of up to 20% on bulk purchases of alcohol. A wholesaler will also allow you to return any bottles of liquor that you have not used. By in large this is a great deal.

LIMIT COCKTAIL HOUR

Having an open bar is quite expensive. You can still show your guests a good time and keep the costs down. The way to do this is to limit the amount of time for the cocktail hour. Once the cocktail hour is over, you can then limit drinks to nonalcoholic beverages or wine. Consider having a host or hostess to pass out the drinks because this helps to prevent waste.

OFF HOUR RECEPTION TIME

We talked a little about this earlier in the book. You can have a breakfast or early afternoon reception and save 30-50% off the reception costs. Breakfast and brunch receptions cost a lot less than dinner receptions do for obvious reasons. Plus, people do not drink as much during the day as they do at night.

SERVE GOOD FOOD NOT EXPENSIVE FOOD

You'll want to go for the lobster and filet mignon meals, however chicken and pasta is just as tasty. Save money by ordering good food, not the most expensive! Also consider having a buffet as opposed to a sit down dinner that costs more.

SERVE EASY HORS D'OEUVRES

Let's face it - you look at some hors d'oeuvres and you just know the cook spent hours in the kitchen making them fancy. Don't worry about that. Your guests just want something to snack on until diner arrives. You can have some prepared that aren't expensive requiring hours of preparation time. Also, avoid using hors d'oeuvres that require expensive ingredients.

SERVE THE GUESTS

You'll want to have someone serve your guests rather than have them helped themselves for several reasons. For one thing, people have a tendency to take too much food before everyone is served. You want to make sure everyone gets at least one heaping helping. The worst thing that can happen at your reception is that everyone doesn't get fed.

USE SMALL PLATES

Your guests won't be able to take too much food if it doesn't fit on the plate. They can always come back for more after everyone is served.

EAT AND THROW IT AWAY

Okay, not everyone is going to love this idea but you can save lots of money by using paper plates, plastic cups and utensils. You can save up 10-20% over the cost of renting breakable china, glasses and silver.

BE PICKY WITH YOUR GUEST LIST

You can keep your costs down by keeping your guest list down. You can invite only family, close friends and business associates and ask your not to bring dates and children.

WAYS TO CREATE A MOOD

Music & All That Jazz

You can cut the cost of music with a little ingenuity. How many of us know someone who knows someone who is as good as professional without actually being one? Yes, that's right. I'm suggesting getting an amateur to play and perform at your wedding. You can save tons of money this way. Take a look at this breakdown.

You can have the friend of a friend or relative of a relative play a musical instrument. It could be a flute, piano or horn. The key to this is to make sure the person is good. Now, you wouldn't want this person to play alone. The cost of your friend's friend will hopefully be nothing. You can have them perform for a short time. Then, you can follow them up with someone who is professional. Someone you do have to pay! The going rates for musicians and singers these days' starts somewhere around $50.00.

Another option is to use the above combination along with some pre-recorded music. This option gives you a little of both worlds. You can even record you own music using high fidelity recording equipment.

A Flower is Just a Flower, Right? Wrong!

Flowers can make your wedding look and feel more romantic and pretty. It used to be a time when white flowers like lily of the valley or orchids and fern was the style. But times have changed! There's nothing wrong with white flowers and fern if that's your style. However, there is a whole new science behind choosing flowers as well as plants that are right for your wedding. You'll want to choose flowers that are in season. Flowers that are in bloom are easier for your florist to get and as a result cheaper as well.

You'll also want to pick fresh flowers that will live longer once they are cut and out of water. Certain flowers hold up better than others. Remember, you have a long day ahead of you that includes picture taking. Your flowers will also have to survive being outdoors in heat or wind. Ask your florist about a hydrator that you can use inside of your bouquet to keep your flowers watered.

If you don't have enough money for live flowers or if your favorite flower is out of season then you may want to think about the unique beauty in silk flowers. The big plus to using silk flowers is that they are less expensive and never die!

You'll want to make a date with the florist to pick out your wedding bouquet. Don't be a horror story where the bride never even saw the flowers before the wedding day. Find a picture of the flowers that you like in a bridal book. You can show the flowers to your florist and hopefully duplicate the bouquet.

Selecting flowers is not just about what looks pretty to you. Flowers have a meaning. All of them d. Isn't it hard to believe that someone actually took the time to make up the different meanings? For instance, did you know that a calla lily means, "magnificent beauty" and the fringed gentian means, "I look to heaven?"

You can create a very special meaning behind the flowers and plants you pick. You can even clue your wedding guests in on the meaning behind your flowers on the back of your wedding program.

Take a look at some of the most popular flowers and what they mean. Put a check by the ones who you like the meaning for and ask your florist to let you see them.

FLOWERS/PLANTS & MEANING

ABUTILON - Meditation
ACACIA (Rose or white) - Elegance, friendship
ACACIA (yellow) - Secret love
ACANTHUS - Artifice, fine arts
ACHILLEA - War
ACONITE - Lustre, misanthropy
ADDER'S-TONGUE - Jealousy
ADONIS - Sad memories
AGRIMONY - Gratitude
ALLSPICE - Compassion
ALMOND (common) - Indiscretion, perfidy
ALOE - Grief, misplaced devotion, religious superstition
ASTOREMERIA - Devotion
ALTHEA - Consumed by love
ALYSSYM (sweet) - Excellence
AMARANTH (coxcomb) - Affection, pretension
AMARANTH (globe) - Constant, unchangeable
AMARANTH - Foppery, immortality, pretension
AMARYLLIS - Beautiful, timid, proud
AMBROSIA - Love returned

ANEMONE - Fading hope
ANGELICA - Inspiration, magic
APOCYNUM - Falsehood, figment, I doubt you
APPLE-BLOSSOM - Preference
ARBOR-VITAE (American) - Immortality
ARBOR-VITAE - I never change, live for me
ARBUTUS - You only do I love
ASCLEPIAS - Sorrowful remembrance
ASH – Prudence, with me you are safe
ASMINE (night-blooming) - Love's vigil
ASPEN - Excess of sensibility, fear
ASTER (China) - Afterthoughts, love of variety
AURICULA (scarlet) - Pride
AURICULA - Painting, wealth is not always happiness
AZALEA - Your blush has won me
BACHELOR'S BUTTON - Devotion, hope, love
BALM - Social intercourse, sympathy
BALSAM - Impatience
BAY-LEAF - I change but in death
BABY'S BREATH - Pure of heart
BAYBERRY - Discipline
BEGONIA - Deformity
BELLFLOWER - Constant
BETONY - Surprise
BITTERSWEET - Platonic love
BLUEBELL - Constant
BLUEBOTTLE - Delicacy
BLUETS - Contentment
BORAGE - Talent
BRAMBLE - Holiness
BROOM - Humility
BRYONY - Prosperity
BURDOCK - Importunity
BUTTERCUP - Riches

BUTTERFLY-WEED - Let me go
CACTUS - Grandeur, warmth
CALLA LILY - Magnificent beauty
CALYCANTHUS - Benevolence
CAMELLIA (Red) - Unpretending excellence
CAMELLIA (White) - Perfected loveliness
CHAMOMILE - Energy in adversity
CANDYTUFT - Indifference
CANTERBURY BELLS - Gratitude
CARDINAL-FLOWER - Distinction
CARNATION - Fidelity, love
CARNATION PINK - Woman's love
CATALPA - Beware of the coquette
CATCHFLY - Unchanging friendship
CATTLEYA - Mature charms
CEDAR - I live but for thee
CELANDINE - Joys to come
CENTAURY - Delicacy
CEREUS (night-blooming) - Transient beauty
CHERRY-BLOSSOM - Spiritual beauty
CHESTNUT-BLOSSOM - Do me justice
CHICKWEED - Rendezvous
CHICORY - Frugality
CHRYSANTHEMUM (Chinese) - Loveliness
CHRYSANTHEMUM (red) - I love
CHRYSANTHEMUM (white) - Truth
CINERARIA - Always delighted
CISTUS - Popular
CITRON - Natured beauty
CLEMATIS - Mental Beauty
CLIANTHUS - Self-seeking, worldliness
CLOTBUR - Rudeness
CLOVER (four-leafed) - Be mine
CLOVER (white) - Think of me

CLOVES - Dignity
COLTSFOOT - Justice shall be done
COLUMBINE - Folly
CONVOLVULUS - Uncertainty
CORCHORUS - Return quickly
COREOPSIS - Always cheerful
CORIANDER - Hidden worth
CORN-BLOSSOM - Riches
CORN-COCKLE - Peerless and proud
CORNEL - Success crowned you
CORNFLOWER - Delicacy, refinement
COWSLIP - You are my divinity
COXCOMB - Foppery
CRABAPPLE-BLOSSOM - Irritability
CRANBERRY - Cure for heartache
CREEPING CEREUS - Modest genius
CRESS - Power, stability
CROCUS - Mirth
CROWN IMPERIAL - Pride of birth
CURRANT - Your frown will destroy me
CUSCUTA - Meanness
CYCLAMEN - Diffidence
DAFFODIL - Unrequited love, regard
DAHLIA - Forever thine
DAISY (colored) - Beauty
DAISY (Michaelmas) - Farewell
DAISY (white wild) - I will think of it
DAISY - Innocence
DANDELION - Love's oracle
DAPHNE - Fame, glory
DARNEL - Vice
DEW-PLANT - Serenade
DIOSMA - Your simple elegance charms me
DITTANY OF CRETE (white) - Passion

THE ULTIMATE WEDDING SAVINGS GUIDE

DOCK - Patience
DODDER OF THYME - Baseness
DOGBANE - Falsehood
DOGROSE - Pleasure
DOGWOOD - Forgetfulness, love undiminished by
EGLANTINE - Genius, I wound to heal, poetry, talent
ELDER - Compassion, zealousness
ENDIVE - Frugality
ESCHSCHOLTZIA - Do not refuse me
EUPATORIUM - Delay
EYEBRIGHT - Cheer up
ENNEL - Strength, worthy of praise
FERN - Fascination, magic, sincerity
FIG - Argument, I keep my secret
FILBERT - Reconciliation
FIR - Time
FLAX - I feel your kindness
FLEUR-DE-LIS - Message
FLOWER-OF-AN-HOUR - Delicate beauty
FLOWERING ALMOND - Hope
FORGET-ME-NOT - Constancy, true love
FOUR-LEAFED CLOVER - Be mine
FOUR-O'CLOCK - Timidity
FOXGLOVE - Youth
FOXTAIL GRASS - Sporting
FUCHSIA - Confiding love
FUMITORY - Spleen
FURZE - Love for all occasions
GARDEN DAISY - Share your sentiments
GARDENIA - Refinement
GENTIAN (closed) - Sweet be thy dreams
GENTIAN (fringed) - I look to heaven
GERANIUM (dark) - Melancholy
GERANIUM (fish) - Disappointed expectation

GERANIUM (horseshoe) - Stupidity
GERANIUM (Ivy) - Favor
GERANIUM (lemon) - Unexpected meeting
GERANIUM (nutmeg) - Expected meeting
GERANIUM (oak) - True friendship
GERANIUM (pencilled) - Ingenuity
GERANIUM (rose) - Preference
GERANIUM (scarlet) - Comforting
GERANIUM (silver leafed) - Recall
GERANIUM (wild) - Steadfast piety
GERANIUM - Gentility, peaceful mind
GILLYFLOWER - Bonds of affection
GLADIOLUS - Ready-armed
GOLDENROD - Encouragement
GOOSEBERRY - Anticipation
GRANDIFLORA - High-souled
GRAPE (wild) - Charity, mirth
GRASS - Submission
HANDFLOWER - Warning
HAREBELL - Submission
HARLEQUIN - Laugh at trouble
HAWKWEED - Quick-sighted
HAWTHORN - Hope
HAZEL - Reconciliation
HEARTSEASE - Think of me
HEATH - Solitude
HELENIUM - Tears
HELIOTROPE - Eagerness, intoxicated with joy
HELLEBORE - Devotion
HEMLOCK - You will cause my death
HEMP - Fate
HIBISCUS - Delicate beauty
HOLLY - Domestic happiness
HOLLYHOCK - Ambition

HONEY-FLOWER - Love sweet and secret
HONEYSUCKLE (coral) - Fidelity
HONEYSUCKLE - Bonds of love
HOP - Injustice
HORNBEAM - Ornament
HORSE-CHESTNUT - Luxury
HOUSELEEK - Vivacity
HOUSTONIA - Contentment
HYACINTH (purple) - Jealousy
HYACINTH (white) - Modest loveliness
HYACINTH - Constancy
HYDRANGEA - Boaster
HYSSOP - Cleanliness
ICE-PLANT - Your looks freeze me
IRIS (German) - Aflame
IRIS Message - Eloquence
IVY - Fidelity Friendship, marriage, wedded love
JACOB'S-LADDER - Come down
JASMINE (cape) - I am too happy
JASMINE (Carolina) - Separation
JASMINE (Indian) - I attach myself to you
JASMINE (Spanish) - Sensuality
JASMINE (white) - Amiability
JASMINE (yellow) - Grace and elegance
JASMINE - I am too happy
JONQUIL - I desire a return of your affection
JUDAS-TREE - Unbelief
KINGCUP - Riches
LABURNUM - Forsaken, pensive beauty
LADY'S SLIPPER - Capricious beauty
LADY'S SMOCK - Ardor
LADY'S THIMBLE - Submission
LADY'S-TRESSES - Bewitching grace
LANTANA - I am unyielding

LARCH - Boldness
LAUREL (ground) - Perseverance
LAUREL (mountain) - Ambition
LAUREL - Perfidy
LAURESTINE - I die if neglected
LAVENDER - Acknowledgment
LEMON - Discretion
LETTUCE - Cold-hearted
LICHEN - Solitude
LILAC (purple) - First love
LILAC (white) - Youthful innocence
LILY (water) - Purity of heart
LILY (calla) - Maiden modesty, beauty
LILY (day) - Coquetry
LILY (frog) - Disgust
LILY (tiger) - I dare you to love me
LILY (white) - Purity and sweetness
LILY (yellow) - Flirtation
LILY-OF-THE-VALLEY - Return of happiness
LINDEN Conjugal - Love
LIVE-OAK - Liberty
LIVERWORT - Confidence
LOBELIA - Arrogance
LOCUST - Affection beyond the grave
LONDON-PRIDE - Frivolity
LOTUS - Estranged love
LOVE-IN-A-MIST - Perplexity
LOVE-LIES - Hopeless but not heartless
LUCERNE - Life
LUPINE (rose) - Fanciful
LUPINE (white) - Always happy
LUPINE - Voraciousness
MAGNOLIA - Nobility
MISTLETOE - Kiss me

MOSS - Charity
MYRTLE - Love
NARCISSUS - Stay as Sweet as You Are
NASTURTIUM - Conquest, Victory in Battle
OLEANDER - Caution
ORANGE BLOSSOM - Eternal Love
ORCHID - Beautiful Lady
ORCHID (CATTLEYA) - Mature Charm
PALM LEAVES - *Victory and Success*
PEONY - Happy Life and Marriage
PETUNIA - Your Presence Sooths Me
PINE - Hope
POPPY (GENERAL) - Imagination
POPPY (RED) - Pleasure
POPPY (WHITE) - Consolation
POPPY (YELLOW) - Wealth, Success
PRIMROSE - I Can't Live Without You
PRIMROSE (EVENING) - Inconstancy
ROSE (BRIDAL) - Happy Love
ROSE (DARK CRIMSON) - Mourning
ROSE (HIBISCUS) - Delicate Beauty
ROSE (LEAF) - You May Hope
ROSE (PINK) - Perfect Happiness
ROSE (RED) - Love, I Love You
ROSE (TEA) - I'll Remember Always
ROSE (THORNLESS) - Love at First Sight
ROSE (WHITE) - Innocence and Purity
ROSE (WHITE AND RED MIXED) - Unity
ROSE (WHITE-DRIED) - Death
ROSE (YELLOW) - Try to Care
ROSEBUD - A Heart Innocent of Love
ROSEBUD (RED) - Pure and Lovely
ROSEBUD (WHITE) - Girlhood
ROSEBUD (MOSS) - Confessions of Love

ROSES (Bouquet of Mature Blooms) - Gratitude
ROSES (Single Full Bloom) - I Love You
SMILAX - Loveliness
SNAPDRAGON - Gracious Lady
SPIDER FLOWER - Elope with Me
STEPHANOTIS - Happiness in Marriage
STOCK - You'll Always Be Beautiful to Me
SWEETPEA - Thank You for a Lovely Time
TULIP (GENERAL) - Perfect Lover
TULIP (RED) - Believe Me
TULIP (VARIEGATED) - Beautiful Eyes
TULIP (YELLOW) - There's Sunshine in Your Smile
VIOLET - Modesty
VIOLET (BLUE) - I'll Always Be True
VIOLET (WHITE) - Let's Take a Chance
ZINNIA (MAGENTA) - Lasting affection
ZINNIA (MIXED) - Thinking of an absent friend
ZINNIA (SCARLET) - Constancy
ZINNIA (WHITE) - Goodness
ZINNIA (YELLOW) - Daily Remembrance

Can you find a flower, maybe two or three out of all of these that you'd like to have in your wedding because of the meaning? There is a rhyme and reason behind picking a flower type. But, there is also a reason why you should be choosy over the size of your bouquet. You want your flowers to add to the beauty of your dress. You don't want your flowers to overwhelm you. Your flowers should accentuate your waistline when you're holding them.

Finally, when choosing a flower it's not just the looks and meaning that are important. They should smell good as well. Gardenias, tuberoses, and peonies are some of the most fragrant smelling flowers.

Chapter 5: Don't Rely on Friends and Family for Video & Photography

Wedding Savings Trend #4

More and more couples are using black and white film for their wedding pictures. If that trend doesn't suit your fancy, you can always put a one-time use color camera on the reception tables and let your guests help to be the photographer.

You should look into hiring a professional videographer and photographer. You can still save you hundreds of dollars off of your videographer/photographers rates while preserving the memories. Think about the last wedding that you attended. What was special about it?

Chances are if you're having a tough time remembering the highlights, then the couple is as well. That's why photographs and video are so important. You may remember that the cake tasted good. You may remember that Uncle Bob made a drunken fool of himself. You made a hit out of Barbara Straisand's "Memories." Nothing plays as well and for so long as video and photographs.

SKIMPING WITHOUT MISSING A SHOT

Most couples decide to have a videographer and a photographer at the wedding. It can be very expensive hiring both. The professional rates begin around one-hundred dollars an hour. Many feel it's worth because there's nothing like a person with an "eye" that knows what to look for in pictures.

Let's go over the pros and cons of still and video shots.

Videotape

The popularity of having a videotape of your wedding has grown throughout the years. One of the best things about video is that you can see the product right away. A skilled videographer actually shoots the video and edits the shot as he goes along. Professional shooters call this video "raw" footage. You can get a copy of the video right after your wedding. However, you can also have the footage cut into a nice video packaged piece. A wedding video package can range starting at up to $2,500. The price includes the cost of the videographer, tape and 2-3 copies.

Photographs

A videotape may give you immediate access to your wedding memories, however still photos are good to have as well. The trends show that couples are sticking with this more traditional way to preserve memories. In fact, they are paying more and more for it.

An average wedding package includes 4 8X10's, forty 4X5's and a leather album. Wedding photographer can cost you as much as $1,500 per event. You can get other photographs for an additional price. A good photographer and videographer will help you to capture the moment without being intrusive to you and guests.

There's an easy way to help make sure that you receive all the pictures that you want on your wedding day. It's called a shot sheet to pass on to your photographer. This sheet will ensure that you get all the right still and video pictures.

40 POINT - PHOTOGRAPHY/VIDEO SHOT SHEET

Before Wedding
1. Morning sunrise
2. Bride gets ready the morning of wedding with bridesmaids
3. Nervous groom waits

Ceremony
1. Bride with bouquet
2. Bride and father walking up the aisle
3. Kneeling in prayer
4. The lighting of the unity candle
5. The exchange of vows
6. The first kiss
7. The couple walking down the aisle.

After Ceremony
1. Bride and groom with parents
2. Bride with her mother
3. Groom with his mother
4. Bride with her father
5. Groom with his father
6. Bride with her grandparents
7. Groom with his grandparents
8. Bride with the children in wedding
9. Groom with the children in wedding
10. Bride with bridesmaids
11. Groom with groomsmen

12 Bride with groomsmen
13 Groom with bridesmaids
14 Bride with maid or matron of honor
15 Groom with best man
16 The entire wedding party

Reception
1 Food
2 Special decorations
3 Couple arrives at reception
4 The couple's first dance
5 The bride dancing with her father
6 The groom dancing with his mother
7 The best man's toast
8 The cake cutting
9 The couple feeds each other
10 Rings
11 Brides bouquet toss
12 Bride and whoever caught the bouquet
13 Groom takes off the brides garter
14 Groom's garter toss
15 Groom and whoever caught the bouquet
16 Bride and groom leaving reception
17 Bride and grooms drive away

CHAPTER 6: PLANNING YOUR HONEYMOON

Wedding Savings Trend #5

Have you heard about honeymoon registries? That's right. Honeymoon registries actually allow gift givers to help pay for your honeymoon through their contributions. Gift givers can also pay for certain activities for you in advance while you're on your honeymoon. What a great idea, huh? And to think, it saves you some money as well. Let's see what would you rather have a third toaster or a scuba diving lesson?

THE EARLY BIRD

If you follow the wedding planning calendar that I've outlined later in this chapter, then you will see that you should start planning the honeymoon early. Consider working with a travel agent who can help you figure out the best trip for you. They also can give you discounts based on their high sales volume. Travel agents are also experts on the trends in the business so they can help you find the best deal.

You should look for an agent that specializes in cruises if you want to go on that type of honeymoon. If you don't want to use a travel agent, then you can also check out the tourist office in the place where you want to honeymoon to get free hotel and activities information.

Next let's look at a 13-Step Guide to Finding Red Light Honeymoon Specials:

Book the Trip Online

It doesn't matter if you're booking a trip several months ahead of time or last minute in a lot of cases if you book your trip online. You can find some really great deals this way. There are several websites that you can find that offer these deals. Check out the resource guide at the end of the book for more information.

Shop for the Honeymoon, Before It

You may hear people talking about waiting to buy once you get to your honeymoon destination. I can tell you that prices are always inflated for tourists. You don't want to wait to shop. Start looking around for bargains before the big day. You'll be glad you did. You can usually find good deals on film, batteries, toiletries, etc. ahead of time.

Shop for the Honeymoon, During It

I just told you how to save money before the honeymoon. Now, let's talk a little bit about how you can save money during the honeymoon. I suggest that you visit many stores during your day out on the town. Simply shop around before settling on any one item.

You'll find prices vary from store to store. In a lot of cases, the stores carry the same merchandise because there are certain items that are unique to that part of the world. Shop around during your honeymoon for the best prices and don't be afraid to try to barter the sales people down.

Plan an Off Season Honeymoon

Who wants to go to Jamaica in the height of summer? Who wants to go to Europe in the fall? Who in the world would ever dream of going to Australia in the winter? You do, that's who especially if it means saving hundreds of dollars! Here's something important to note. Off-season doesn't necessarily mean bad weather. A lot of people assume it does.

Off-season simply means that fewer people are traveling to these destinations for a variety of reasons. It could have something to do with the end of summer break and the beginning of the school year. It's really hard to tell in some cases. However, the important thing to note for you is that there are advantages to planning an off-season honeymoon.

One of the biggest advantages is you'll get cheaper prices on hotel and airfare. That's because there are fewer people traveling during off-season. You'll also get better service from cab drivers, tour guides, hotel and restaurant employees, etc. They'll just be glad to see you around because the crowds won't be around.

Cheaper Destinations

Going to a cheaper destination does not mean that you won't have a good time. Places like Mexico and Canada are more affordable based on their low currency rates. Other places like the Bahamas and Jamaica are so frequently traveled that it has helped to bring down the rates. Choosing a cheaper destination could be an economically healthy alternative for you.

Close to Home

There are several advantages to staying close to home for your honeymoon. You save time, money and a lot of hassle that comes from traveling if you drive. I know a lot of couples that were able to upgrade to better accommodations because they decided to drive to a local resort.

Eat Smart

Here's a tip that very few penny pinchers ever think about. There's always that "must eat at" restaurant in every travel destination. It's usually a five star restaurant with great food, service and high prices. Well, try eating at this place for lunch instead of dinner.

Lunch prices are usually more affordable. Plus, if you don't like the food, then you won't be stuck with a high tab. If you like the food, then say what the heck! Splurge! Go back for dinner, but let it be your choice to spend the big bucks, not theirs. Also, don't forget to ask about Happy Hours. It's another great way to have fun and save money.

Use Alternative Travel Plans

Instead of taking a plane, why not ride the rails? The train is a cost effective alternative to flying. If you're not honeymooning too far from home, then taking a scenic bus ride may be nice as well. You can plan to make several stops along the way to make the trip more exciting if you're going a long distance.

Frequent Flier Miles

This is a great way to get to your honeymoon destination if you have the miles saved up. While you're at it, check into other membership rewards that might come along with hotel and car rentals as well.

Air Pass

This option is available on airlines that service some of the foreign destinations like Europe and South America. These tickets let you travel to different countries as long as they are within a certain region. Trying to get a good deal on an air pass is well worth the effort.

Some hotels and airlines are offering great deals to people who make their reservations online. Some sites like priceline.com actually lets you pick your own price as long as your travel day, time and place to stay are flexible.

All Inclusive an All Around Good Deal

All-inclusive are a great deal for people who want to pay for it and enjoy their honeymoon worry free. Most all-inclusive package deals cover the room, meals, drinks and entertainment. Also covered is tours, taxis, taxes and tips as well? Be sure to find out what an all-inclusive covers because it varies from one company to another.

Condo or Villa It!

If you pick this cost saving measure, you can save a pretty penny on meals. Oh, so you don't want to cook on your honeymoon. The upside to a condo or villa is the romantic meals with candlelight and low music. Get the picture now? Choosing this option is NOT all work!

Hotels Offer Great Deals

They don't advertise this deal so you'll have to call around to check on prices. You can have your reception at some hotels and they'll throw in a honeymoon suite free. You can also get discounts on rooms for your guests.

HONEYMOON BUDGET SWEET 'N SIMPLE

Let's turn from saving money on your honeymoon costs to tracking and planning your exact honeymoon costs. You may be thinking okay; I know what my budget is. It's $1,000. End of subject. Well, it's not so easy. In order for you to meet your $1,000 budget, you have to have everything itemized. This section will help you to do that.

Let's break it down:

EASY TO TABULATE HONEYMOON BUDGET TABLE.

MAJOR TRANSPORTATION

Air, Rail, or Ship	_____
Rental Car	_____
Gas	_____
Taxi & Tips	_____
Total Transportation	_____

ACCOMMODATIONS

Hotel	_____
Resort	_____
Services (Spa, Dry Cleaners)	_____
Total Accommodations	_____

FOOD

Breakfast (daily x number of days)	_____
Lunch (daily x number of days)	_____
Dinner (daily x number of days)	_____
Snacks (daily x number of days)	_____
Total Meals	_____

THE ULTIMATE WEDDING SAVINGS GUIDE

ENTERTAINMENT
Theater & Concerts   _____
Nightclubs   _____
Sightseeing   _____
Athletic Rental   _____
Total Entertainment   _____

GIFTS & SOUVENUERS   _____

TOTAL BUDGET (Add totals) _____

Chapter 7: Your Planning Timeline

> **Wedding Checklist:**
> ☐ Set your budget
> ☐ Find a place
> ☐ Start the guest list
> ☐ Reserve the date and venues
> ☐ Book an officiant
> ☐ Find a photographer
> ☐ Find a florist
> ☐ Find a caterer

Wedding Savings Trend #6

The best is saved for last! This is the savings trend of all savings trends! Get married over Thanksgiving Dinner. Or, Christmas. The Fourth of July even! More and more couples are opting this as a way to kill two birds with one stone. You don't have to worry about paying for a reception hall if you don't want to. You don't have to worry about paying for extra food if you don't want to! I believe this is the ULTIMATE wedding savings trend.

Below is a Four Month Wedding Countdown Calendar. Follow the time suggestions on this calendar to keep your planning organized and stress free as possible.

THE WEDDING COUNTDOWN CALENDAR

FOUR MONTHS and counting

1. Finish making plans for the reception
2. Finish the guest list

3. Order invitations and thank you notes
4. Order wedding cake
5. Select a photography/videography plan
6. Select a floral and music
7. Select the food menu

THREE MONTHS and counting

1. Write out the wedding ceremony
2. Write out your own vows if you want
3. Reserve tuxedos
4. Make a doctor's appointment to get blood tests
5. Start addressing invitations

TWO MONTHS and counting

1. Mail invitations
2. Write thank you notes for any gifts you've received so far
3. Make a shot list for the videographer and photographer
4. Start practicing hairstyles
5. Pick the music

ONE MONTH and counting

1. Get a marriage license
2. Place a wedding announcement in the newspaper
3. Address wedding announcements for people who aren't coming to wedding
4. Write thank you notes for gifts you've already received
5. Set a date for the final fitting of the wedding dress
6. Loosen your wedding shoes up by wearing them around the house
7. Buy luggage if you don't already have
8. Plan rehearsal dinner

THREE WEEKS and counting

1. Double check to make sure everyone is measured for tuxedo
2. Finalize rehearsal and rehearsal dinner plans
3. Choose transportation for wedding party on wedding day

TWO WEEKS and counting

1. Confirm the reception guest list with caterer
2. Give photographer and videographer a shot list
3. Pack for the honeymoon
4. Determine wedding ceremony, reception and rehearsal dinner seating

ONE WEEK and counting

1. Confirm the arrangements
2. Florist, caterer, photographer
3. Honeymoon, bridal suite, airline tickets, travelers checks.
4. Final fitting of wedding gown
5. Bridesmaids luncheon
6. Confirm rehearsal plans

Planning a wedding doesn't need to be stressful and overwhelming. And you don't have to be rich to plan an elegant wedding. You don't have to be the most organized person, either. Just follow the guidelines and suggestions from this book and you'll be living a life in love forever after.

Here's to you and a happy future together!

Chapter 8: Wedding Resources

BRIDAL CONSULTANTS

Association of Bridal Consultants
(860) 355-0464
www.bridalassn.com

BRIDAL REGISTRIES

Macy's Wedding Channel
www.MACYS.WEDDINGCHANNEL.COM

Neiman Marcus
www.neimanmarcus.com

Target
(800) 888-9333
www.target.com

The Home Depot
www.homedepot.com

WEDDING INVITATIONS

www.weddingbells.com

WEDDING VIDEOGRAPHY

Wedding and Event Videographers Association International (WEVA) 800 501-WEVA
www.weva.com

WEDDING WEBSITES

www.brides.com

www.bridesave.com
www.theknot.com
www.todaysbride.com
www.ultimatewedding.com
www.weddingchannel.com

EXPERTS ON RELIGIOUS REQUIREMENTS

Beth Din of America (Jewish)
www.bethdin.org

Church of Jesus Christ of Latter Day Saints (Mormon)
http://www.lds.org

Evangelical Lutheran Church in America
www.elca.org

General Council Assemblies of God
www.ag.org

Greek Orthodox Archdiocese of America
www.goarch.org

Presbyterian Center, News Services Office
www.pcusa.org

Quaker Information Center
www.afsc.org/qic.htm

Union of American Hebrew Reform (Jewish/Reform)
www.uahc.org

Unitarian Universalist Association
www.uua.org

BUSINESS CHECK

Council of Better Business Bureaus
www.bbbonline.org

Consumer Information Center
www.pueblo.gsa.gov

FLOWERS

Teleflora (Free brochures)
www.teleflora.com

VIDEOGRAPHER AND PHOTOGRAPHY

Professional Photographers of America, Inc.
www.ppa.com

Wedding and Portrait Photographers International
www.wppi-online.com

WEDDING MUSIC

American Federation of Musicians
www.afm.org

American Society of Composers, Authors and Publishers
www.ascap.com

WEDDING REGISTRY'S

Crate & Barrel
www.crateandbarrel.com

Honeymoon Registry Websites
www.thehoneymoon.com

Target Stores
www.target.com

Tiffany & Co.
www.tiffany.com

Williams-Sonoma
www.williams-sonoma.com

WEDDING TRAVEL

www.travel.state.gov

Amtrak
www.amtrak.com

Consumer Reports Travel Letter
www.consumerreports/org/services/travel.html

Cruise Lines International Association
www.cruising.org

Travel Health Services
www.travelhealth.net

Meet the Author

April Hall came to wedding planning naturally as she was fascinated with weddings at a young age and preferred bridal and wedding magazines over age appropriate magazines such as Teen Beat and Seventeen. April will tell you she doesn't like to be called a planner or consultant. She prefers to be called a wedding producer because she takes a couple's dreams and produces the magical event that far surpasses merely planning or advising. April began planning weddings when she was still in college and applied for her first business license before she graduated. April's attention to detail and her dedication to her couples along with her exceptional customer service that embraces family and guests alike has made her services and reputation one of a kind and in demand.

April's undergraduate degree in Art and her MBA guarantee that she has the creative skills for beautiful dreams and the business skills to manage a budget and get a complex event produced on time. When April isn't creating fairy tale weddings, she enjoys spending her time with her husband, her two energetic sons and two equally energetic dogs.

April Hall has been creating wedding magic for over 15 years as she grows and enhances her business and has developed customer relationships that have seen her produce multiple weddings from the same families. April Hall is a wedding producer extraordinaire!

MORE BOOKS BY APRIL HALL

Wedding Planning for the Bride-to-Be: Your Guide to an Organized and Memorable Wedding

www.ingramcontent.com/pod-product-compliance
Ingram Content Group UK Ltd.
Pitfield, Milton Keynes, MK11 3LW, UK
UKHW022219230426
12048UKWH00016BA/944